CONSERVATORY CANADA

T0078899

Guitar Technique Book
Grades 1 to 10

Containing the Grade by Grade technical requirements
of Scales, Triads & Arpeggios

for

Conservatory Canada examinations in guitar

Prepared by

KEVIN LOVE

ISBN 978-1-49500-523-7

Novus Via Music Group Inc.
189 Douglas Street, Stratford, Ontario, Canada N5A 5P8
(519) 273-7520 www.NVmusicgroup.com

Contents

Grade One

- All technical tests must be played from memory, evenly, with good tone, logical fingering.
- Metronome markings should be regarded as *minimum* speeds.

SCALES

- To be played from memory.
- Scale fingerings: Right hand fingered i-m, using rest or free stroke at the candidate's choice.
- Number of octaves as written.

MAJOR ♩=92

MINOR (Harmonic) ♩=92

MINOR (Melodic) ♩=92

CHROMATIC ♩=92

TRIADS

- To be played from memory.

MAJOR ♩=92

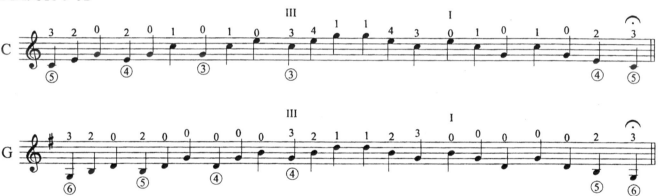

MINOR ♩=92

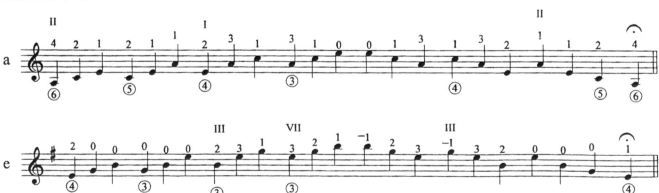

Grade Two

- All technical tests must be played from memory, evenly, with good tone, logical fingering.
- Metronome markings should be regarded as *minimum* speeds.

SCALES

- To be played from memory.
- Scale fingerings: Right hand fingered i-m, using rest or free stroke at the candidate's choice.
- Number of octaves as written.

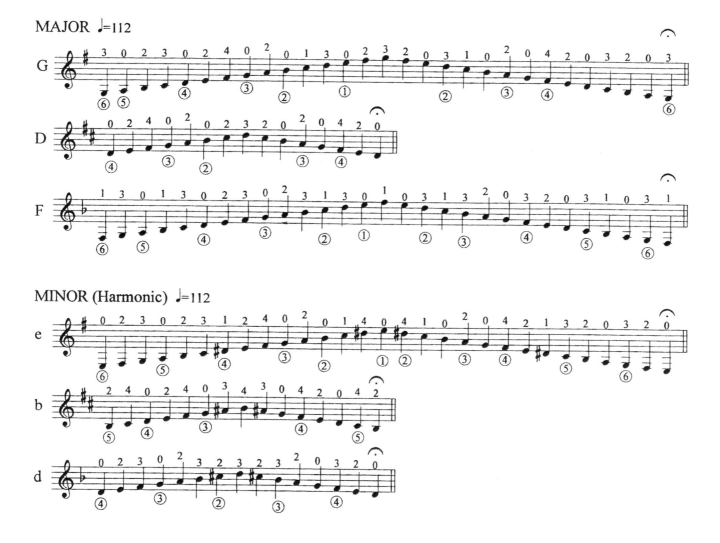

CHROMATIC ♩=112

TRIADS

- To be played from memory.

Grade Three

- All technical tests must be played from memory, evenly, with good tone, logical fingering.
- Metronome markings should be regarded as *minimum* speeds.

SCALES

- To be played from memory.
- Scale fingerings: Right hand fingered i-m or m-a (to be specified by the examiner), using rest or free stroke at the candidate's choice.
- Number of octaves as written.

MAJOR ♩=120

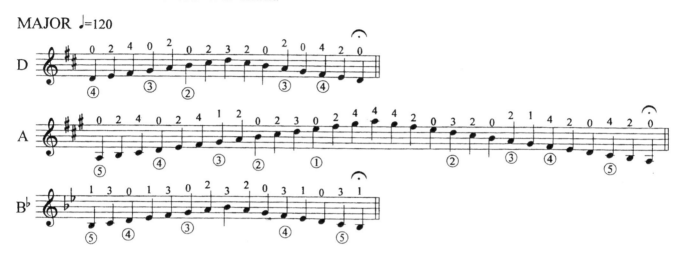

MINOR (Harmonic) ♩=120

MINOR (Melodic) ♩=120

CHROMATIC ♩=120

TRIADS

• To be played from memory.

MAJOR ♩= 50

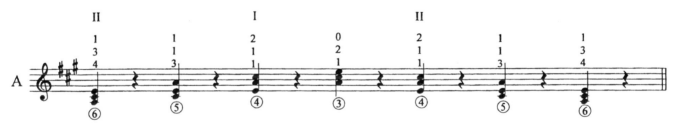

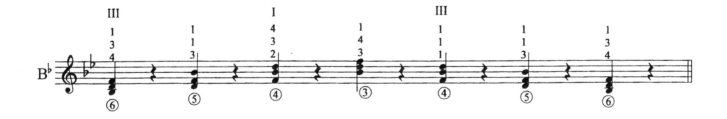

MINOR ♩= 50

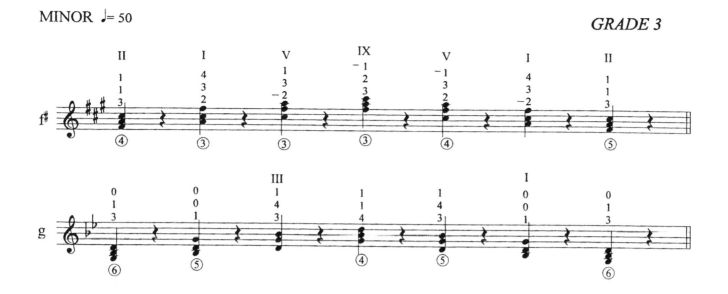

ARPEGGIOS

● To be played from memory.

MAJOR ♩= 60

MINOR ♩= 60

Grade Four

- All technical tests must be played from memory, evenly, with good tone, logical fingering.
- Metronome markings should be regarded as *minimum* speeds.

SCALES

- To be played from memory.
- Scale fingerings: Right hand fingered i-m, m-a, or i-a (to be specified by the examiner), using rest or free stroke at the candidate's choice.
- Number of octaves as written.

MAJOR ♩=72

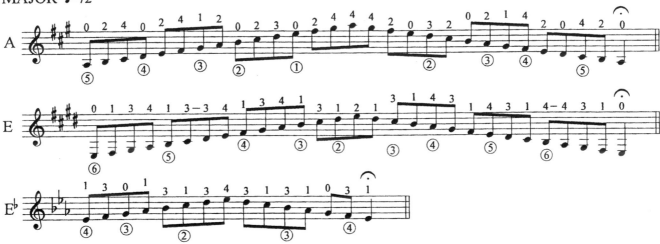

MINOR (Harmonic) ♩=72

MINOR (Melodic) ♩=72

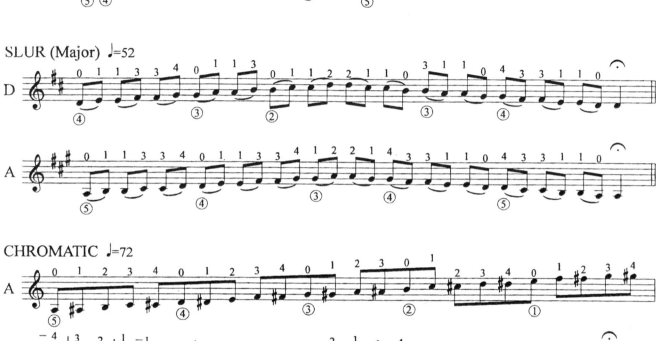

TRIADS

- To be played from memory.

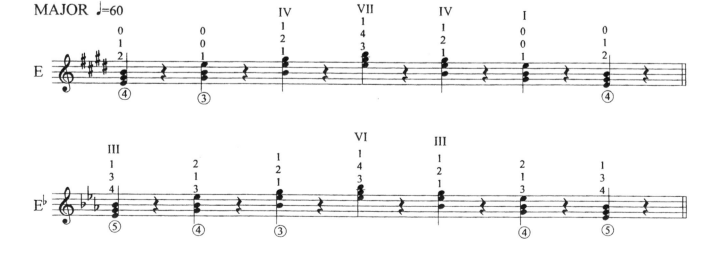

9

MINOR ♩=60

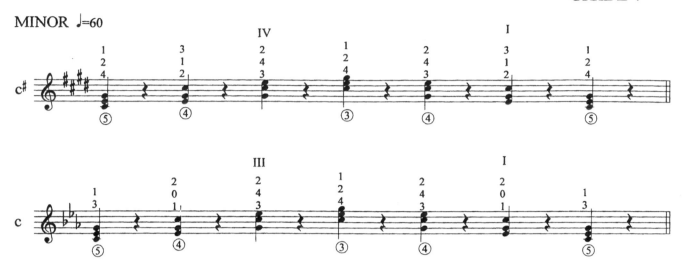

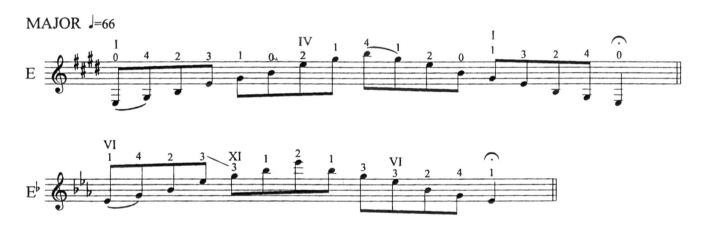

ARPEGGIOS

● To be played from memory.

MAJOR ♩=66

E

Eb

MINOR ♩=66

C#

C

Grade Five

- All technical tests must be played from memory, evenly, with good tone, logical fingering.
- Metronome markings should be regarded as *minimum* speeds.

SCALES

- To be played from memory.
- Scale fingerings: Right hand fingered i-m,m-a, or i-a (to be specified by the examiner),
  using rest and free stroke. Use only movable, closed string left-hand fingering (except open 6th string).
- Number of octaves as written.
- Review scales may be fingered as in grade 4.
- Note that each scale should be prepared in **both** sixteenths and triplet eighths.

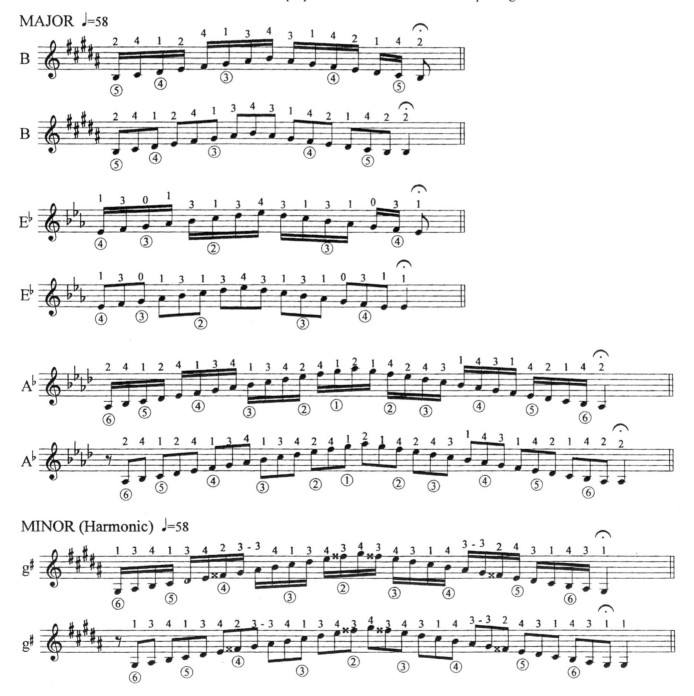

MINOR (Melodic) ♩=58

REPEATED NOTE (Major) ♩=84

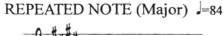
B — one octave

E♭ — one octave

A♭ — two octaves

All repeated note scales should be played ascending and descending, using appropriate left hand fingerings. The following right hand fingerings may be used:

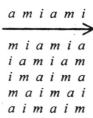

a m i a m i

→

m i a m i a
i a m i a m
i m a i m a
m a i m a i
a i m a i m

REPEATED NOTE (Melodic Minor) ♩=84

g♯ — two octaves

c — one octave

f — two octaves

SLUR (Major) ♩=66

CHROMATIC ♩=66

13

WHOLE TONE ♩=88

TRIADS

- To be played from memory.

MAJOR ♩=72

MINOR ♩=72

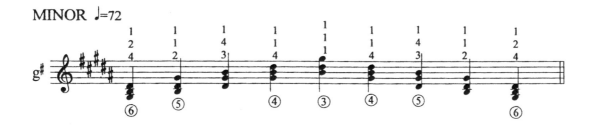

ARPEGGIOS

- To be played from memory.

MAJOR ♩=72

MINOR ♩=72

DOMINANT 7th ♩=72

Grade Six

- All technical tests must be played from memory, evenly, with good tone, logical fingering.
- Metronome markings should be regarded as *minimum* speeds.

SCALES

- To be played from memory.
- Scale fingerings: Right hand fingered i-m, m-a, or i-a (to be specified by the examiner), using rest and free stroke. Use only movable, closed string left-hand fingering (except open 6th string).
- Number of octaves as written.
- Note that each scale should be prepared in **both** sixteenths and triplet eighths.

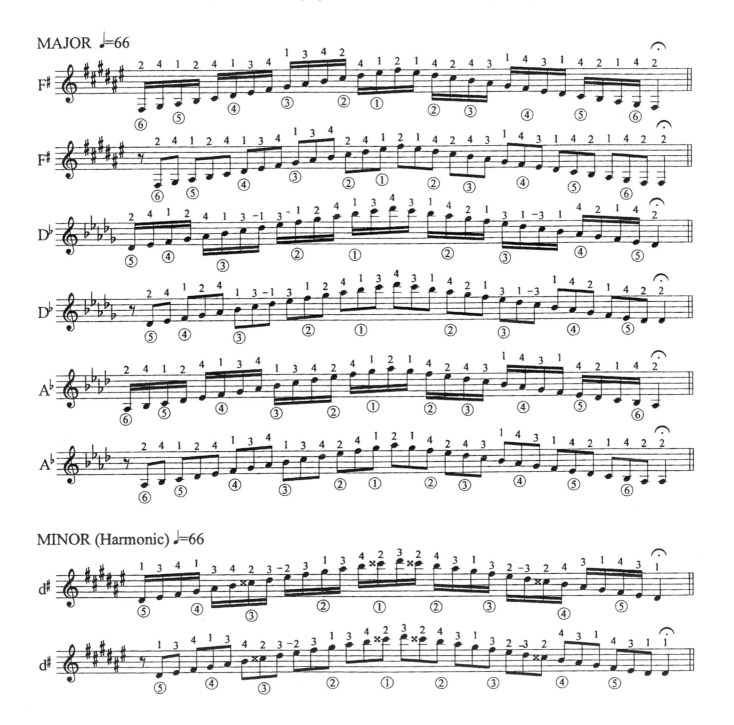

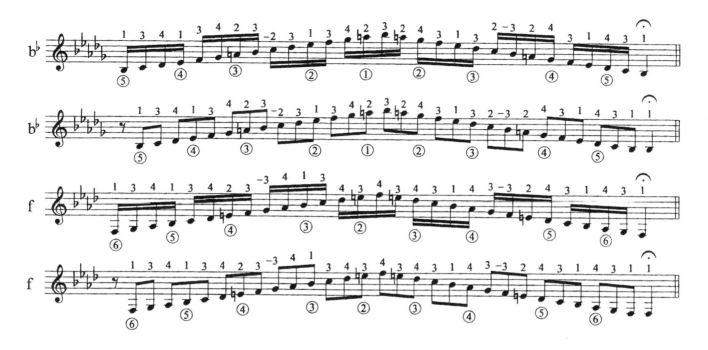

MINOR (Melodic) ♩=66

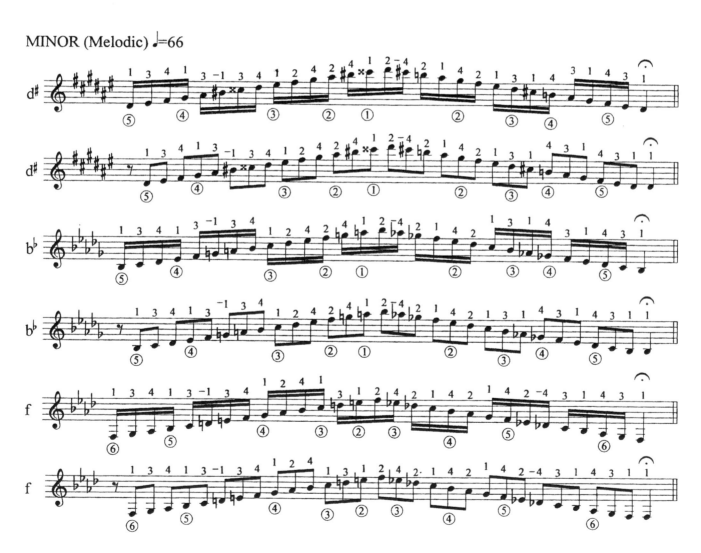

REPEATED NOTE (Major) ♩=72

F♯ — two octaves

D♭ — two octaves

A♭ — two octaves

All repeated note scales should be played ascending and descending, using appropriate left hand fingerings. The following right hand fingerings may be used:

a m i m   a i m i   m a i a

m i m a   m i a i   a i a m
i m a m   i m i a   i a m a
m a m i   i a i m   a m a i

REPEATED NOTE (Harmonic and Melodic Minor) ♩=72

d♯ — two octaves

b♭ — two octaves

f — two octaves

SLUR (Major) ♩=80

D

3rds ♩=60

C

6ths ♩=60

C

CHROMATIC ♩=66

WHOLE TONE ♩=96

BLUES ♩=92

TRIADS

● To be played from memory.

MAJOR ♩=76

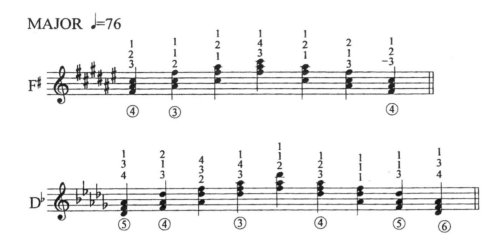

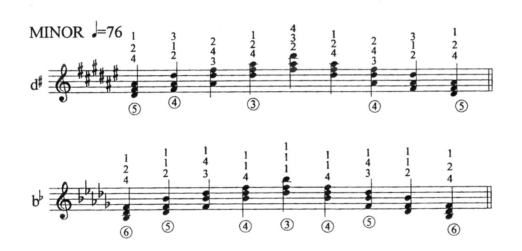

ARPEGGIOS

● To be played from memory.

MAJOR ♩=76

MINOR ♩=76

DOMINANT 7th ♩=76

DIMINISHED 7th ♩=76

Grade Seven

- All technical tests must be played from memory, evenly, with good tone, logical fingering.
- Metronome markings should be regarded as *minimum* speeds.

SCALES

- To be played from memory.
- Scale fingerings: Right hand fingered i-m, m-a, or i-a (to be specified by the examiner),
  using rest and free stroke. Use only movable, closed string left-hand fingering (except open 6th string).
- Number of octaves as written.
- Note that each scale should be prepared in **both** sixteenths and triplet eighths, as in the following
  example.

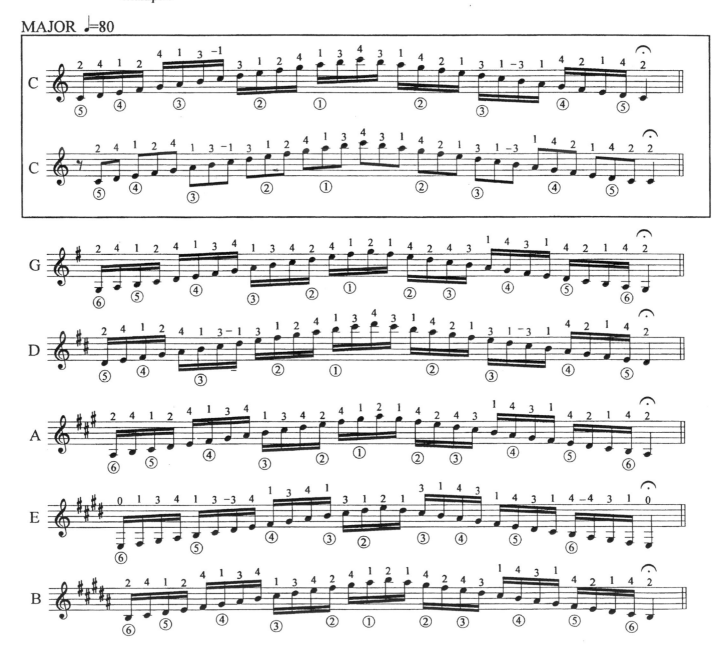

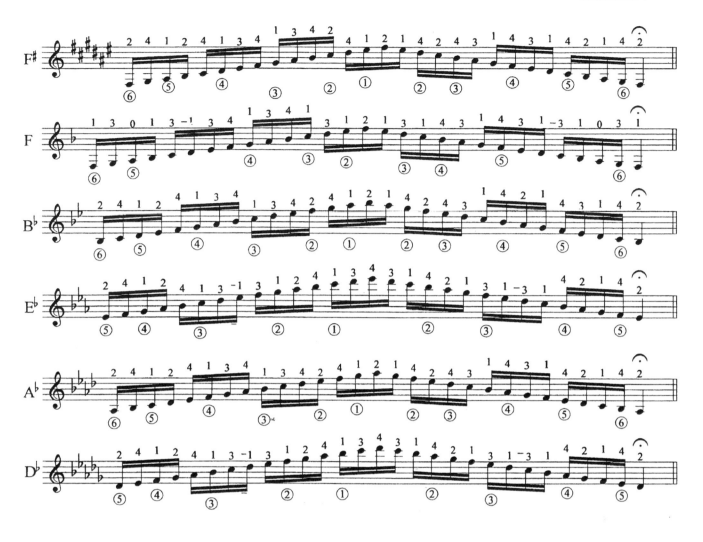

MINOR (Harmonic) ♩=80

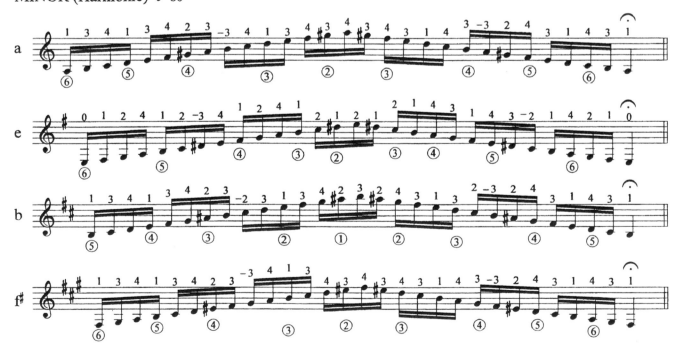

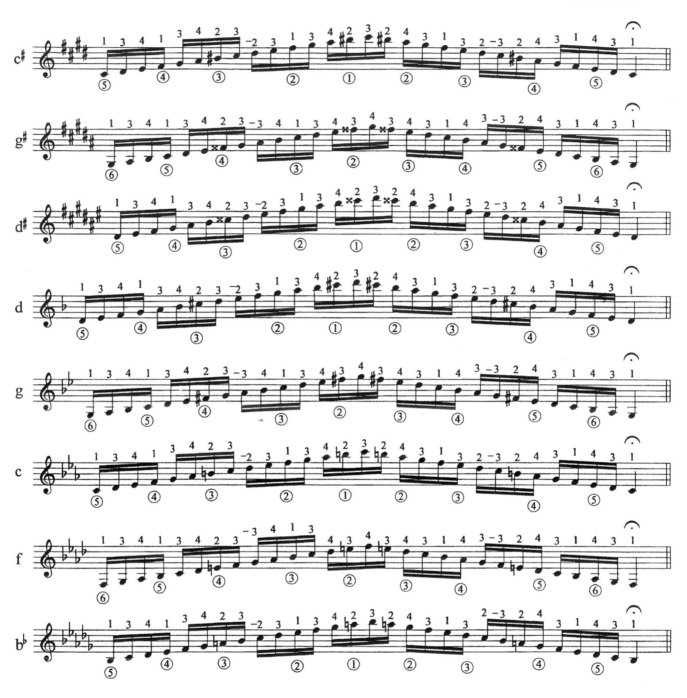

MINOR (Melodic) ♩=80

REPEATED NOTE (Major) ♩=72

B — two octaves

F# — two octaves

Db — two octaves

All repeated note scales should be played ascending and descending, using appropriate left hand fingerings. The following right hand fingerings may be used:

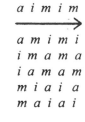

a i m i m

a m i m i
i m a m a
i a m a m
m i a i a
m a i a i

REPEATED NOTE (Minor) ♩=72

g# — two octaves

d# — two octaves

bb — two octaves

SLUR (Major) ♩=104

3rds ♩=66

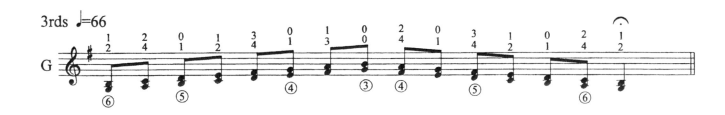

6ths ♩=66

26

CHROMATIC ♩=80

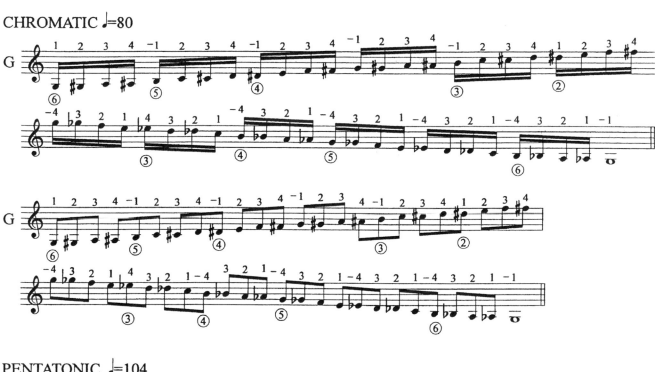

PENTATONIC ♩=104

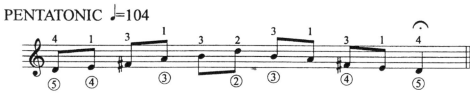

BLUES ♩=104

TRIADS

- To be played from memory.

MAJOR ♩=80

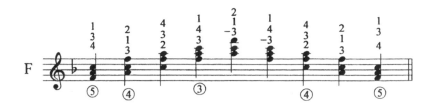

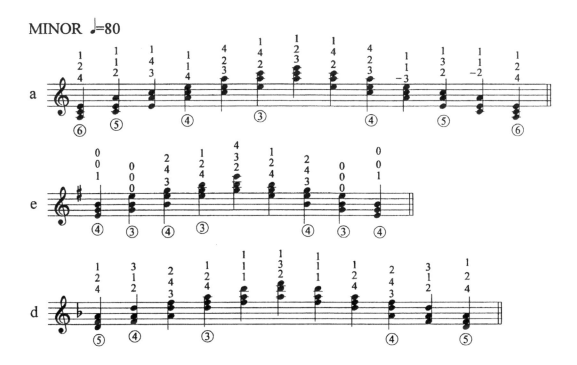

MINOR ♩=80

ARPEGGIOS

- To be played from memory.

MAJOR ♩=80

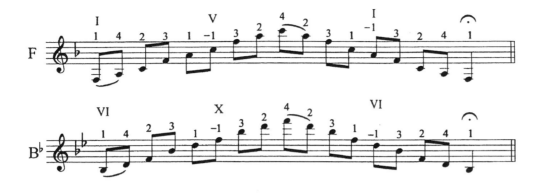

MINOR ♩=80

DOMINANT 7th ♩=80

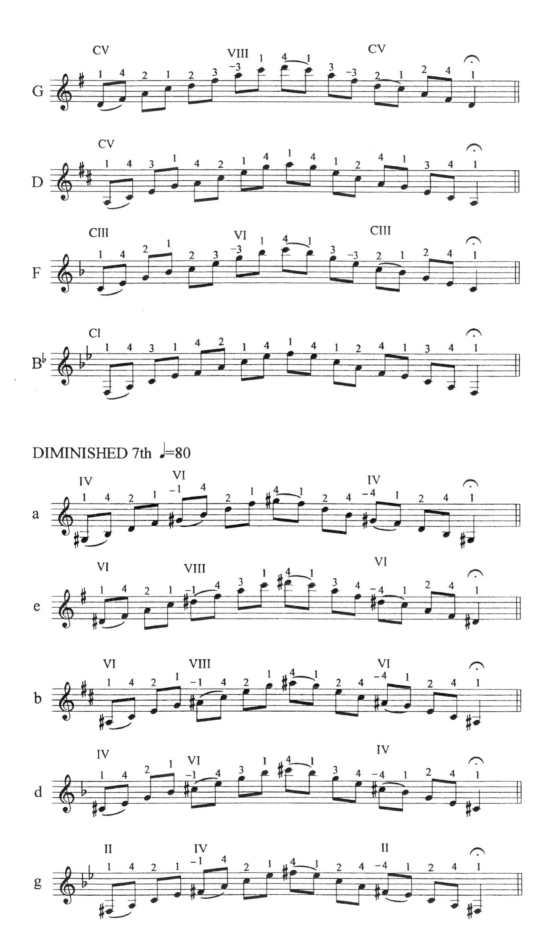

DIMINISHED 7th ♩=80

Grade Eight

- All technical tests must be played from memory, evenly, with good tone, logical fingering.
- Metronome markings should be regarded as *minimum* speeds.

SCALES

- To be played from memory.
- Scale fingerings: Right hand fingered i-m, m-a, or i-a (to be specified by the examiner), using rest and free stroke. Use only movable, closed string left-hand fingering (except open 6th string).
- Number of octaves as written.
- Note that each scale should be prepared in **both** sixteenths and triplet eighths, as in the following examples of two and three octave scales.

MAJOR ♩=92

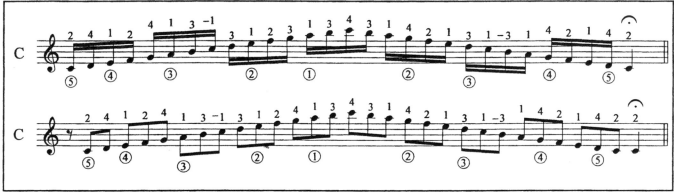

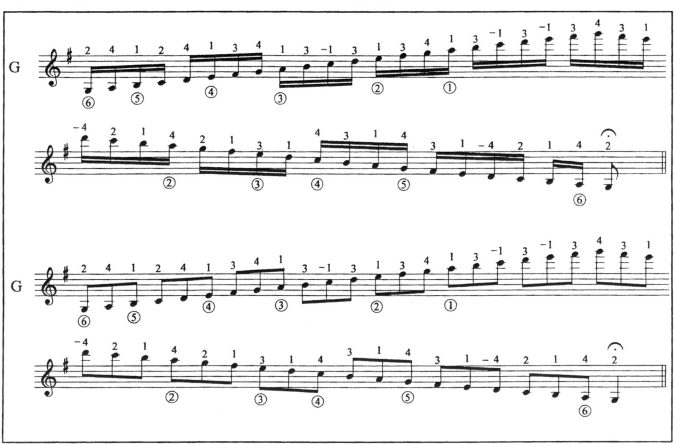

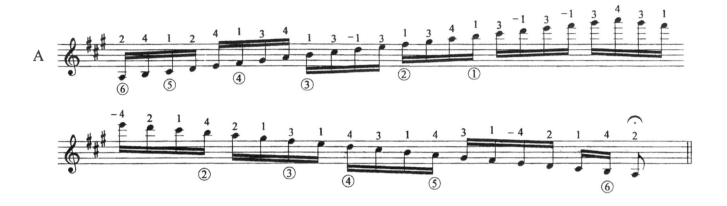

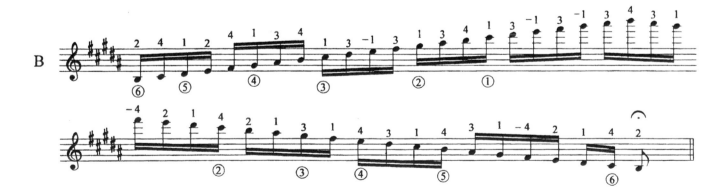

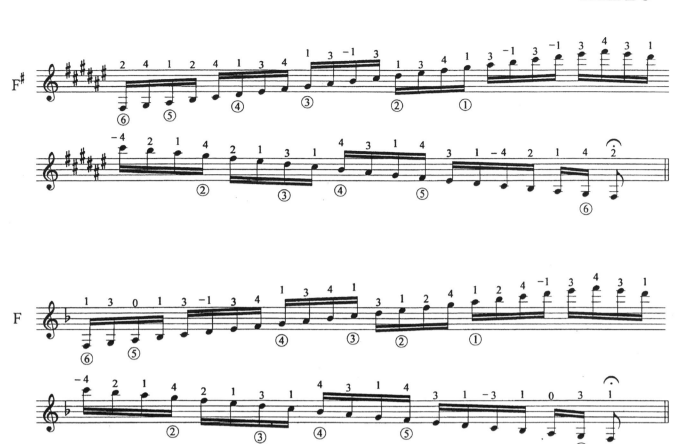

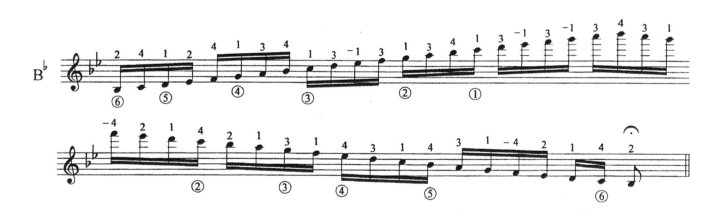

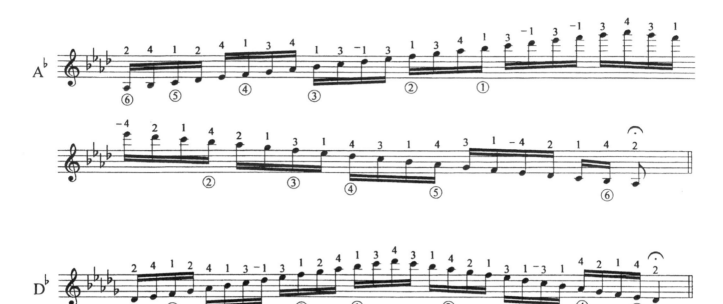

MINOR (Harmonic) ♩=92

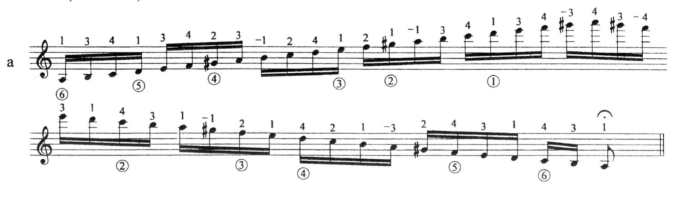

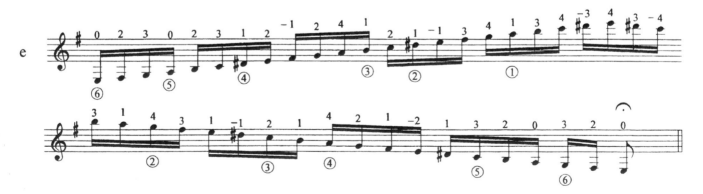

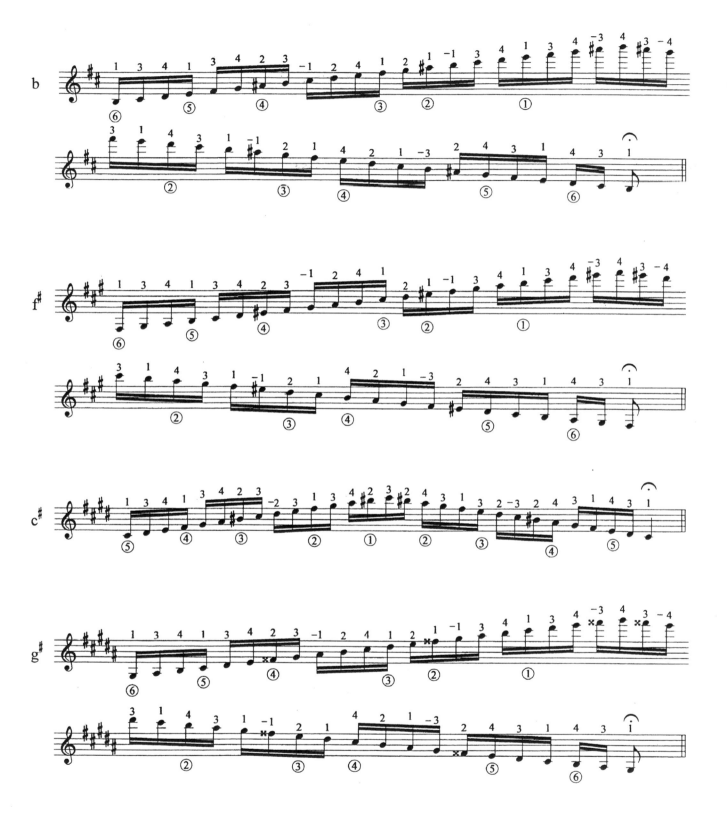

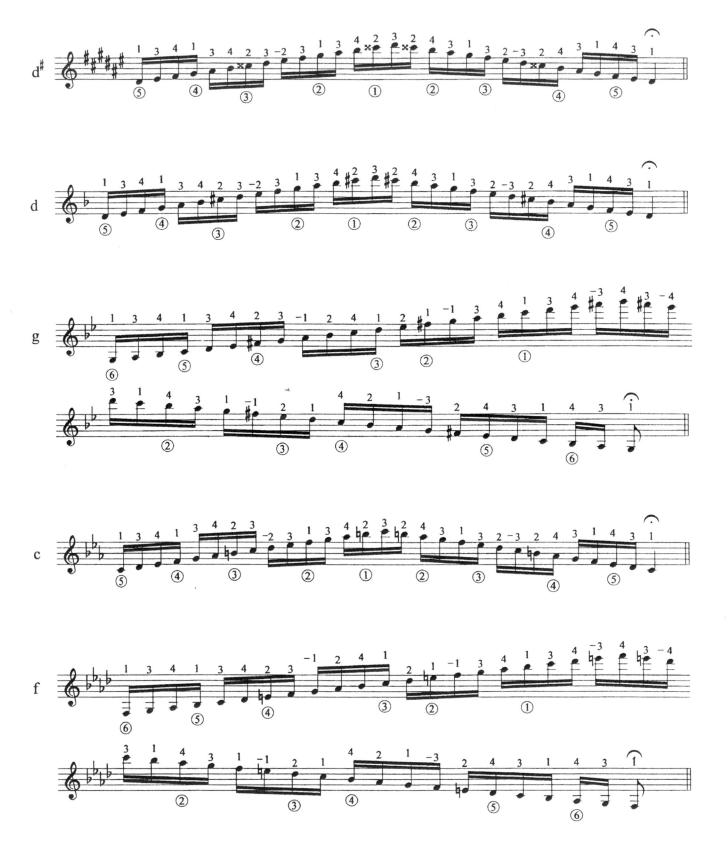

36

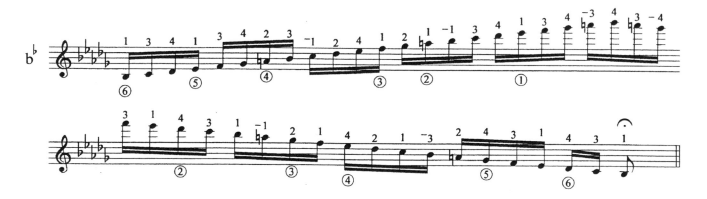

MINOR (Melodic) ♩=92

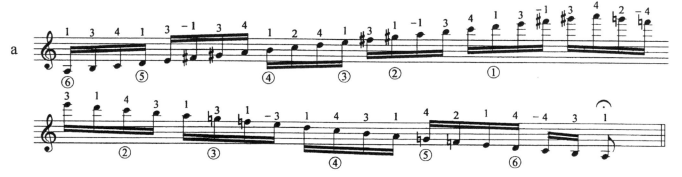

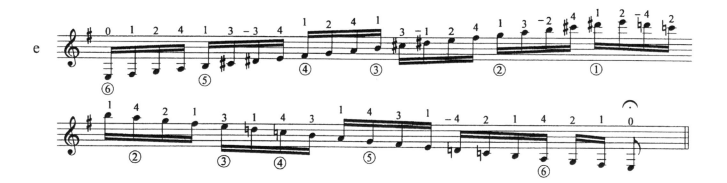

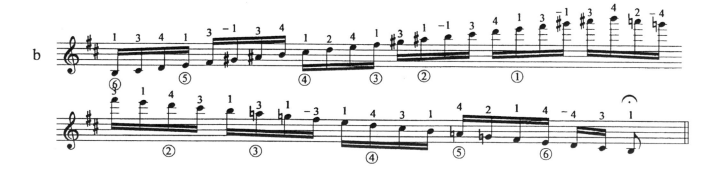

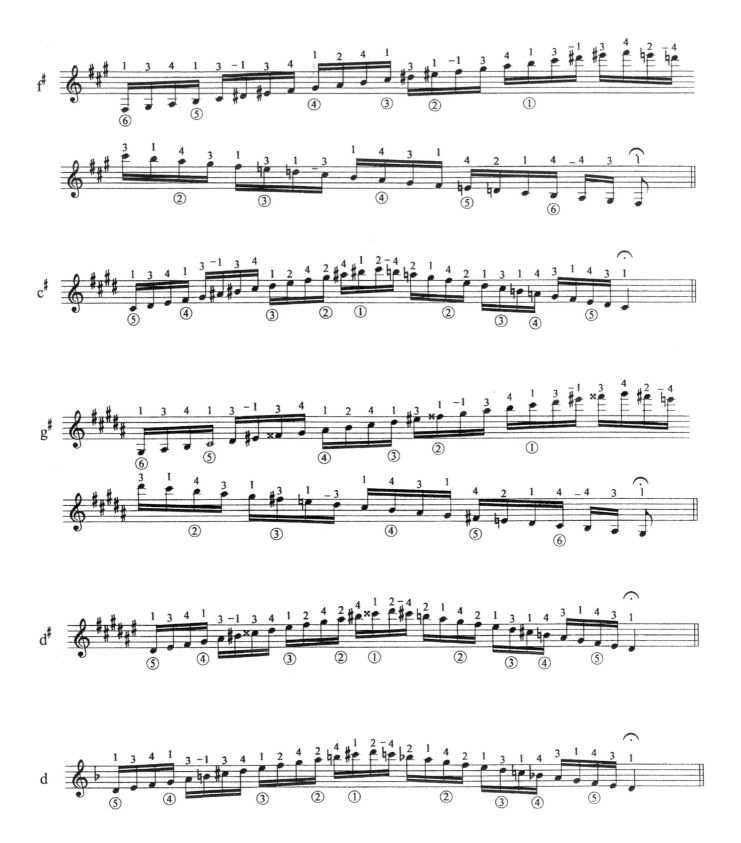

g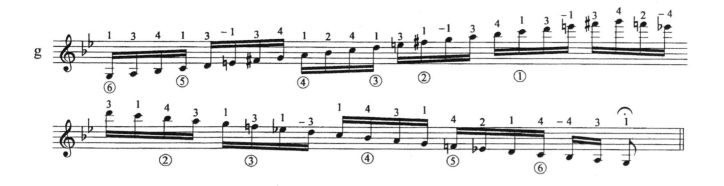

c

f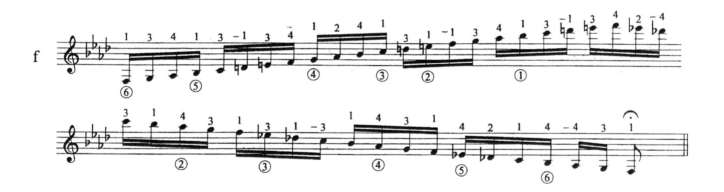

b♭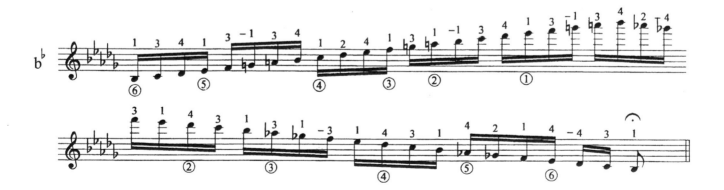

REPEATED NOTE (Major) ♩=69

C   two octaves

All repeated note scales should be played ascending and descending, using appropriate left hand fingerings. The following right hand fingerings may be used:

a i m i m i   m i a i a i
→
a m i m i m   m a i a i a
a m i a m i
i m a m a m
i a m a m a
i m a i m a

REPEATED NOTE (Minor) ♩=69

a   two octaves

SLUR (Major) ♩=116

C

A

3rds ♩=80

D

Broken 3rds ♩=80

D

40

WHOLE TONE / HALF TONE ♩=112

TRIADS

• To be played from memory.

MAJOR ♩=84

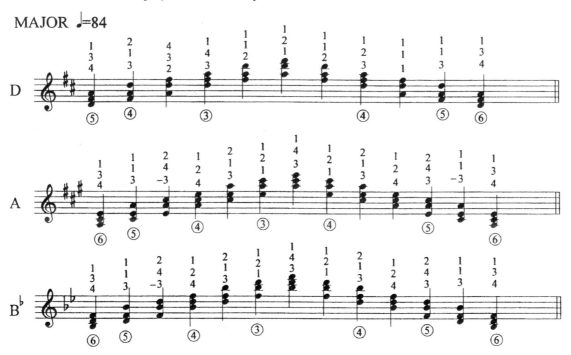

MINOR ♩=84

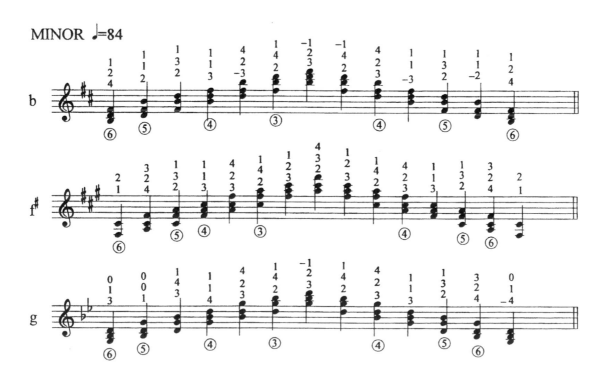

ARPEGGIOS

• To be played from memory.

MAJOR ♩=92

A

E

B

E♭

A♭

MINOR ♩=92

f♯

DIMINISHED 7th ♩=92

DOMINANT 7th ♩=92

Grade Nine

- All technical tests must be played from memory, evenly, with good tone, logical fingering.
- Metronome markings should be regarded as *minimum* speeds.

SCALES

- To be played from memory.
- Scale fingerings: Right hand fingered i-m,m-a, or i-a (to be specified by the examiner),
  using rest and free stroke. Use only movable, closed string left-hand fingering (except open 6th string).
- Number of octaves as written.

MAJOR ♩=104

- ALL KEYS
- in sixteenth notes AND in triplet eighth notes (as in Grade 8)

MINOR (Harmonic AND Melodic) ♩=104

- ALL KEYS
- in sixteenth notes AND in triplet eighth notes (as in Grade 8)

REPEATED NOTE MAJOR ♩=76

- ALL KEYS
- in quintuplet sixteenth notes AND in sextuplet sixteenth notes.

REPEATED NOTE MINOR (Harmonic AND Melodic) ♩=76

- ALL KEYS
- in quintuplet sixteenth notes AND in sextuplet sixteenth notes.

SLUR MAJOR ♩=132

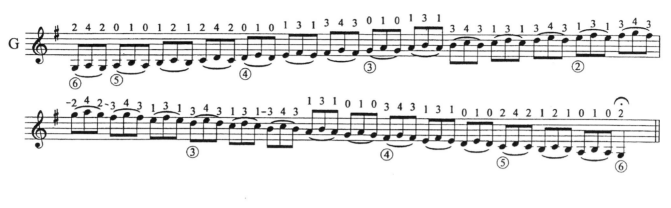

3rd & 6th(Solid & Broken) MAJOR ♩=88

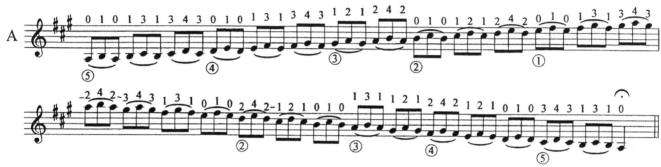

CHROMATIC ♩=104

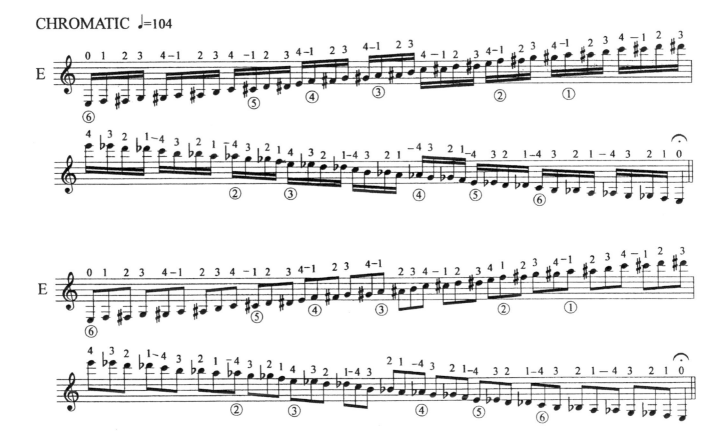

ARPEGGIOS

MAJOR, MINOR, DOMINANT 7th, DIMINISHED 7th ♩=96

- ALL KEYS
- in eighth notes (as in Grade 8)

Grade Ten

- All technical tests must be played from memory, evenly, with good tone, logical fingering.
- Metronome markings should be regarded as *minimum* speeds.

SCALES

- To be played from memory.
- Scale fingerings: Right hand fingered i-m,m-a, or i-a (to be specified by the examiner), using rest and free stroke. Use only movable, closed string left-hand fingering (except open 6th string).
- Number of octaves as written.

MAJOR ♩=112

- ALL KEYS
- in sixteenth notes AND in triplet eighth notes (as in Grade 8)

MINOR (Harmonic AND Melodic) ♩=112

- ALL KEYS
- in sixteenth notes AND in triplet eighth notes (as in Grade 8)

REPEATED NOTE MAJOR ♩=84

- ALL KEYS
- in quintuplet sixteenth notes AND in sextuplet sixteenth notes.

REPEATED NOTE MINOR (Harmonic AND Melodic) ♩=84

- ALL KEYS
- in quintuplet sixteenth notes AND in sextuplet sixteenth notes.

SLUR MAJOR ♩=144

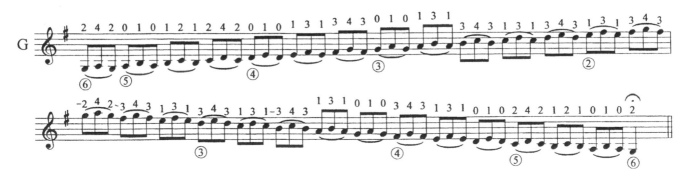

3rd & 6th(Solid & Broken) MAJOR ♩=104

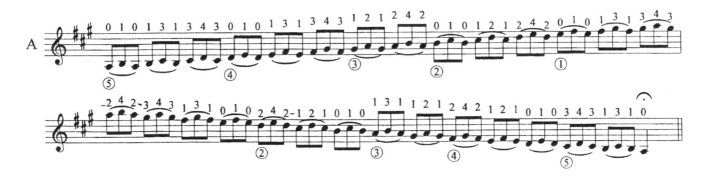

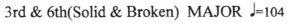

CHROMATIC ♩=112

ARPEGGIOS

MAJOR, MINOR, DOMINANT 7th, DIMINISHED 7th ♩=104

- ALL KEYS
- in eighth notes (as in Grade 8)

CONSERVATORY CANADA™

CONSERVATORY CANADA™ conducts accredited music examinations in both Classical and Contemporary Idioms™ in many disciplines throughout Canada—from grades/levels 1 to 10 on through to professional Associate and Licentiate Diplomas.

For information about CONSERVATORY CANADA™ and our examination programs, please contact:

Office of the Registrar
Conservatory Canada
45 King Street, Suite 61
London, Ontario, Canada
N6A 1B8

Telephone: 519-433-3147
Toll free in Canada: 1-800-461-5367

Fax: 519-433-7404

Email: officeadmin@conservatorycanada.ca

www.conservatorycanada.ca